IMAGES
of England

BEFORE THE
CHANNEL TUNNEL

The Misses Marchant, Rachel (left) and Ruth (right), from a photograph by Robert Kennelly in about 1931. The location is The Street, Newington with the churchyard wall to the right. The girls are wearing the uniform of Kent College, Folkestone.

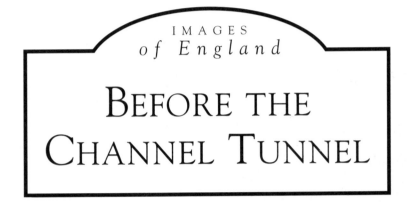

IMAGES
of England

BEFORE THE
CHANNEL TUNNEL

Compiled by
Paul Crampton

TEMPUS

First published 2001
Copyright © Paul Crampton 2001

Tempus Publishing Limited
The Mill, Brimscombe Port,
Stroud, Gloucestershire, GL5 2QG

ISBN 0 7524 1584 0

Typesetting and origination by
Tempus Publishing Limited
Printed in Great Britain by
Midway Colour Print, Wiltshire

Mr William Marchant, with 'Old Amos' on the right, at Home Farm, Newington in about 1914. That year, Mr Marchant became the farm manager and held this position until retiring in 1930. Shortly after, Home Farm was sold by the Brockman Estate to the Vincents of Pound Farm.

Contents

Acknowledgements

Many of the photographs reproduced in this book are family snaps or amateur pictures never intended for publication. Together they form a unique record of a lost community and are included for their human interest. I would like to thank the following ex-residents for supplying pictures and, or, information (their lost homes are in brackets): Sally Elwood (*Treetops*); David Ivory (*Treetops*); David Oakley (*Its-It*); Anne Seymour (*Braewood*); Heather Tyrell (*Cliff End*); June Philpott (*Cliff End* & Danton Lane Cottages); Wilf Philpott (Danton Lane Cottages); Norman Hall (Danton Lane Cottages) and Ian Warne (Danton Lane Cottages). In addition, I am also grateful to the following for information and pictures: Peter Hooper; Paul Grundy; Suzanne Royd-Taylor; Tom Oakley; Mrs Thomas; Brian Hart; Peter Bamford and the Folkestone and District Local History Society, Canterbury Archaeological Trust, in particular Richard Cross; Andrew Savage and Rupert Austin; and also Camille Newell of Eurotunnel. Finally, I would like to express my heartfelt gratitude to three special ladies without whom this book would not have been possible: To Janet Adamson of Folkestone Library and Museum, who allowed us unlimited access to the archives and has been helpful and encouraging throughout. To Miss Rachel Marchant, life long resident of Newington for providing so many invaluable and personal memories, for bringing the Kennelly material to life and generously providing tea and chocolate biscuits whilst we pored over the old pictures. Lastly to my wife Mary Anne, for her unfailing love, support and enthusiasm throughout the period of the research, interviews and 'now' pictures in 1997 and 1998, then overcoming personal tragedy to help pull all the fragments together, enabling me to compile this finished book.

Children from Newington and Peene pose for the camera of Robert Kennelly in Buckwells Meadow, in the early 1930s. The Elham Valley Railway embankment and Peene Bridge can be seen behind.

Introduction

I never intended to write books about anywhere other than Canterbury and certainly not the Channel Tunnel! When the scheme seemed like it was finally going ahead in 1986, I, along with most of the population of Kent, was opposed to the idea of a tunnel. By this time, my photographic collection of the lost buildings of Canterbury was already well under way. I was also taking my own pictures of city buildings under threat of demolition, but had not as yet had anything published. Another of my interests, since childhood, was railways and especially those in Kent. Therefore, as soon as the 'Chunnel' plans were announced, I felt it important to record what was left of the Elham Valley Railway, that once crossed the proposed terminal site. Consequently, in February 1988, I set out for Peene with naturalist Leigh Gillett. The surviving brick buttresses of the railway bridge constructed above the road from Newington was my starting point. (Leigh's interests lay in the ponds and streams near the former line, which were known to be inhabited by great crested newts). The old railway embankment east of Peene, with its well preserved occupation arches, made a fine subject for my camera. Through one of the old railway arches, I noticed a group of distant buildings at the foot of the Cheriton Downs. This was the hamlet of Danton Pinch and I could see a footpath leading from the arch in front of me straight to it. However, by this time, we had unwittingly already strayed onto the area recently secured by contractors Transmanche Link (hereafter referred to as TML), prior to the construction of the terminal. My passion for photographing buildings soon to be demolished, overcame my concern that we may be trespassing, so I took a closer look.

Prudence dictated that we approach Danton Pinch more discreetly, so we retraced our steps along the embankment and drove from Peene via Hill Road to Danton Lane. It was barricaded at the top, albeit only half-heartedly, so we decided to walk down. The perfectly intact, but empty houses and bungalows of Danton Pinch, presented a fascinating, yet eerie scene that captured my imagination. I photographed most of the buildings, whilst Leigh dabbled in some of the garden ponds for botanical and amphibious treasures. We then wandered down Danton Lane towards Danton Farm, being completely ignored *en route* by the massive earth graders that were already plying to and fro. Danton Lane Cottages, boarded up and with their gardens already destroyed, were as far south as we dared go. Before going home, I photographed Stone Farm on the A20 and vowed to return for more pictures. Thus started a twelve year on-and-off project to take and trace pictures of the lost scenes and buildings of the Channel Tunnel Terminal site. When Mary Anne and I married in 1997, the book project really took off. We began to track down the former residents of those lost buildings and record their personal stories. Research in Folkestone library, greatly assisted by Janet Adamson, led us to discover the Robert Kennelly archive, a charming collection of bucolic photographs taken around Newington between 1929 and 1935. There is no doubt that Robert Kennelly was something of an enigma. Little was known of his background, and the circumstances of his arrival in the Newington area in the mid 1920s are as vague as his disappearance some time in the late 1930s. It is thought that his early years may have been spent in the Folkestone area and that he later moved to Canada. During the First World War, he served with the Canadian forces. Lifelong Newington resident, Miss Rachel Marchant, told us that he came to stay in nearby Peene after having been invalided out of the army. He always walked with his left arm bent behind his back, which may have been as a result of his war injuries. For Miss Marchant, his arrival always heralded the start of summer, as he would return to the area at the same time every year. No one knew where he went for the rest of the year, neither did they dare ask. During his stay, he always lodged with Harry Amos and his wife Emily at No. 5 Peene Cottages. Miss Marchant first met Robert Kennelly whilst out for a walk with her father, in around 1926. He had a very distinctive appearance, tall and thin, and he walked with a stoop. This elusive migrant always carried a plate glass camera slung over one shoulder and was never seen without a walking stick. Local people estimated his age to be somewhere between fifty and sixty years old! He had a deep distinctive voice, as would befit his manner, height and bearing and spoke with a slight Canadian accent. Everyone he met liked him and gladly gave him permission to photograph wherever and whoever he chose. Robert Kennelly never published or exhibited any of his pictures. For him, photography was just a therapeutic hobby; a way of helping to forget his infirmities. His visits to the area ended abruptly just before the Second World War. It is believed that he spent some time in a Folkestone hospital and later died there. He was never known to have married; and nobody is certain whether it was his sister, thought to live in the Folkestone area, who subsequently donated his albums of photographs to the town Library, or not. The pictures Kennelly took of Newington, Peene and the people who lived there in the 1920s and 1930s, stand as more than just a record of a way of life long since vanished. They perfectly encapsulate the tranquil years that preceded agricultural mechanisation, the Second World War and the threat of building a Channel Tunnel. Now that the dust has settled, quite literally, following completion of the terminal complex, the view through the photographer's lens is a very different one. What would Robert Kennelly think of his beloved corner of Kent if he saw it now? Today, the Channel Tunnel is a reality and my opinion of it has softened. Yet, when boarding the shuttle on another quest for inexpensive red wine, I cannot help but think of all those people whose lives were irrevocably changed by what must be acknowledged, however grudgingly, as one of the greatest achievements of the twentieth century.

Paul Crampton
January 2001

One
The Kennelly Legacy

Jack Heyman, who was the chief waggoner, is seen here with two of the black Welsh light-weight cart horses owned by the Vincents of Pound Farm, Newington; the site of this photograph. He was always known simply as 'Ayman' and became one of Robert Kennelly's more popular subjects. His grave can be found in Newington churchyard, alongside those of his former employers, the Vincent family.

Rachel Marchant, with her older sister Ruth, in the garden of the Old Vicarage, Newington at the end of August 1931. Rachel was thirteen years old and Ruth, sun-tanned from a recent holiday with her grandparents in Suffolk, was sixteen years old. The Marchant family had lived at the Old Vicarage since 1916. Ruth went on to become a nurse, but died tragically of septicaemia, contracted from a patient. She was only eighteen years old.

Hilda Darby (far left) and her sister Betty (centre) pose with two of their little chums for this charming, yet typical Robert Kennelly set piece. They are on a footpath just off the A20 at Newington. Mr Kennelly always gave plenty of notice for his photographic assignments and would provide the sun bonnets and baskets for his young models.

Rachel Marchant, in her early teens, on the Water Walk in Ashley Wood, Beachborough Park. Her mother had expressed reservations about Mr Kennelly and was concerned that he may have been shell-shocked! However, Miss Marchant said he was always a perfect gentleman and that there was never any suggestion of anything improper about these assignments. He did not pay his models, but rewarded them instead with boxes of *Terrys of York* Plain Chocolates, which Miss Marchant did not like at that time!

A group of local children pose for Mr Kennelly's camera in a field between the villages of Newington and Peene, just north of where the village hall now stands. Amongst the gathering are: Betty Darby, Pat Pearson, Cyril Parker and two of the ten strong Taylor family. The horse and cart both belong to Pound Farm. Just visible between the two farm workers is the railway bridge that carried the Elham Valley Line over the road to Peene.

Pound Farm based worker, Jack Heyman, ploughing at the Brockman's Whitelands Fields, north-east of Peene. Robert Kennelly's pictures of farm life in and around Newington were less rehearsed than those of the village children. Nevertheless, the farm labourers were no less willing to pose for the camera! These sloping fields above Peene, fell outside the area required for the Channel Tunnel Terminal and therefore survive today.

Another Pound Farm worker, Charlie Hammond, busy cutting corn east of Newington in the early 1930s. Other labourers are just visible in the background stacking up the cut sheaves. Today, this area is entirely occupied by the terminal site and only lorries are stacked up these days.

Haymaking in Vicarage Meadow, a wedge shaped tree lined field immediately to the south-east of Newington. Along the field's southern boundary ran the old coach road, known locally as The Grove. At the time, Vicarage Meadow was owned by the Brockmans of Beachborough. The field is now entirely buried beneath a massive embankment which allows road and rail access to the Channel Tunnel Terminal.

Rachel Marchant, astride a cart horse called Violet with Bill Fox from Pound Farm who is holding the reins. They are *en route* to the Old Forge for re-shoeing which stood just west of and opposite the junction with The Street and Ashford Road. Violet was sold to the Marchants by farm owners, the Vincent family.

The Vincent team are in front of the Old Granary at Home Farm during the early 1930s. By this time, the Vincents of Pound Farm had also acquired and were running Home Farm. In front is Mr S. Vincent (senior) with Beryl Godden. Behind, from left to right are: Jack Heyman; G. Cullen; B. Cullen; Jack Jeffery; Wilfred Vincent; Charlie Vincent; Bert Mayatt; Tom White; Jack Glover; Mr Beech; Bob Jeffrey and Bill Fox.

The first visit of the Kent Education Library van to Newington was in 1931. In this photograph it is parked in the driveway of the old village hall, known as 'The Village Hut'. Rachel Marchant is standing on the left of the driver in the peaked cap. In the middle doorway is Mr Fisher, publican of the Barley Mow and behind him Ruth Marchant and Mrs Warman. The lady holding the book is the headmistress Miss Appleton and furthest right, is a group of girls including Betty Darby and Pat Pearson who are standing in the doorway.

Then: Bill Warman (senior) and Jack Heyman are with the ploughing team in a field south of Danton Pinch and east of Newington. Some of the houses in the hamlet of Danton Pinch can just be made out behind the fence. The Warmans lived in a rendered terraced house just off The Street, Newington; which has long since been demolished.

Now: The same location as it was in April 1998. In the distance, lorries are on the freight customer route, queuing to board a shuttle train. The white tower (centre view) is the Folkestone Control Centre, effectively the brains of the whole system. Immediately to the right is part of the passenger customer route toll area and left, the terminal staff car park.

Then: A charming study of Rachel Marchant, taken by Robert Kennelly, when she was about fourteen years old. The stile she is leaning on led from Street Meadow (now the playing field) into Buckwells Field. To the north was Wick Wood, the Elham Valley Line and Peene. Asholt or Ashley Wood was to the west and Newington, the south. Miss Marchant remembers that day as being exceptionally windy and having to anchor her dress down with her knees!

Now: Miss Rachel Marchant in summer 1998 is standing outside her bungalow *Westholme* in Newington. She recalls a wonderful childhood and loved life at home and on the farm. On school days, she could not wait to return home in order to go out into the fields. Just like her late sister Ruth, she had a caring vocation and was the local District Nurse for many years. Miss Marchant lived at the Old Vicarage until 1983, when she moved to *Westholme*, only a few yards away.

Two

Newington

Newington church, pictured from the southwest, sometime in the 1920s. Much of this charming building dates from the late twelfth century, although there is evidence of earlier Saxon and Norman work. When the belfry was built in 1907, the bells were temporarily hung in the churchyard. On the left are two corn stacks standing at the southern end of Home Farm yard. Beyond the stacks and the church is the famous Yew tree, which some locals insist is over 2,000 years old!

Home Farm facing north in the late 1920s, when William Marchant was still farm manager. In the foreground is the Tarred Barn, a thatched ramshackle structure with room enough inside for three horses. The brick gabled building at the far end of the yard is the Cutting Meat House, possibly a corruption of Cutting Mead. Inside it was a mechanical horse-driven device that cut both green and dried fodder.

The Old Granary, Home Farm, looking north-west in about 1930. It faced due east and was situated to the west of the main farmyard. The building remained largely unchanged until the hurricane of October 1987, when it lost most of its original Kent-peg tiles. Current farm owner, Houchin, replaced the lost tiles with much heavier ones. In the autumn of 1997, the Old Granary suddenly collapsed. Whether or not the heavier tiles were a contributing factor is unclear. The ruins were cleared away in June 1998.

The Street, Newington in the late 1920s, just north of the junction with Ashford Road (later the A20). Everything to the left belongs to Home Farm. Just beyond the telegraph pole is the Tarred Barn, which was later demolished by the Vincents following their purchase of the farm. The single storey corrugated iron building was divided into sections and used to house calves. Furthest away is the Old Tithe Barn at the north-east corner of the farm complex.

A Kennelly view of an ancient track, known as the 'T-Path', which runs from The Street to the hamlet of Frogholt. Left, is the Old Tithe Barn of Home Farm. The rendered terrace (right) contains three dwellings. Furthest right is the Easton's private door, who ran the adjacent shop. The home of a retired couple, the Pearsons, was next and around the corner the house belonged to the Warman family. The gabled houses facing the 'T-Path' were occupied by the Bakers and furthest away was occupied by Jimmy Goodburn junior, wood reve for the Brockman Estate.

The symmetrical façade of the five dwellings that make up Church Cottages, as they appeared in the early 1930s. They stand opposite Newington church, at the junction of The Street and School Lane. The cottages were numbered 1 to 5, from right to left. The early 1930s occupants were as follows: The Shorts at No. 5; Miss Sarah Nutley (Mrs Jimmy Goodburns aunt) at No. 4 and the verger, Dick Goodburn (Jimmy Goodburns brother) at No. 3. The tenants of Nos 1&2 were constantly changing.

The humbler looking rear elevation of Church Cottages, also from the early 1930s. As can be seen from this view, and the one above, the arrangement of the doors is quite bizarre. They were built in the late seventeenth century as Poor Law Establishments (or almshouses) for the village of Newington and were owned by the Brockman family. Originally, the toilets were all in a block, one per cottage and numbered 1 to 5 on each door.

An Edwardian period view of the Old Vicarage captured from the southwest corner of the garden. It stopped being a vicarage after 1868, when what would later become Newington Grange was built. The Old Vicarage, as it became, was then divided into two properties, one was the eighteenth century brick-built section nearest the camera and the other, the older and mostly timber framed section at the eastern end. In 1916, the Marchant family purchased the brick section from James Goodburn senior, verger of Newington church.

William Wood was the Brockman Estate shepherd, and is seen here during a visit to William Marchant at the Old Vicarage in around 1926 or 1927. As is evident, the old man had a badly deformed left hand. Behind him is the west elevation of the Old Vicarage. By this time, the Marchants had been able to purchase the timbered east wing from a man called Hopkins and thus, were able to occupy the whole building.

Pound Farm was the name given for both farmhouse and farm. The young men featured in this late 1920s view could well be the farmer's sons, Wilfred and Charles Vincent. Pound Farm was built in stages over four centuries, the oldest parts were the thirteenth century stone rubble walls around the lower part of the west wing (left). The fourteenth-century east wing (right) was once a separate building and only joined to the west wing by a central hall in the fifteenth century.

The back of Pound Farm taken by Robert Kennelly in the early 1930s. The rear elevations give away the true age of the building as they lack the brick skin added to the frontage in the seventeenth century. Various members of the extended Vincent family occupied different parts of the house. By this time, the Vincents worked all the local farmland, adding Longport Farm to their empire in 1927 and Home Farm in 1930.

This early view of The Street looks north and probably dates from the 1890s. It has been included to show the condition of the Smallest Wealden house before alterations were made in the Edwardian period. As the name imples, the house (third from the left) was the smallest known of the Wealden hall type. This term describes a timber-framed house with a central hall, open to the roof, and a two-storey wing at each end. The Smallest Wealden is featured in more detail in the top image on p. 28.

This 1950s view of the same scene, shows the changes that occurred in the intervening years. A pair of Edwardian houses were squeezed in next to the Smallest Wealden, replacing a single storey dwelling, set back from the street frontage. At the far end of the row, the double fronted house was lost, probably in the fire of 1917. Beyond that is the single storey Smithy which eventually disappeared around 1914. On the right, the Pound Farm barn has been replaced by a modern equivalent.

Members of the Canterbury Archaeological Trust work in a trench north of Newington in late 1987. Beyond is the west side of the Pound Farm house. The trust's fieldwork and excavations for Eurotunnel commenced in mid 1987 and prospection trenches were dug in order to evaluate any archaeological materials beneath. The area north of the village was included in the dig; as this is where the terminal's access roads were to be routed, that is, before the eleventh hour switch to the more destructive southern route.

Another view of the many evaluation trenches, this time in Vicarage Meadow and photographed looking in a northeasterly direction. Unlike the trenches north of Newington, where evidence of Saxon occupation was found, nothing of major significance was discovered here. Nestling in the tree lined boundary to Vicarage Meadow is a grounded railway wagon, used to stable any livestock grazing there. Beyond the wagon is one of the Folkestone Rugby Club pitches.

This bleak study of the partly demolished shell of Newington Grange, looking south from The Grove in the winter of 1987 through to 1988. Newington Grange became a victim of the controversial decision to re-route the terminal access roads from the north, to the south of Newington. The consequences of this change are explored more fully in Chapter Three.

The demolished remnants of Stone Farm on the A20, immediately south of Newington are all that was left of the buildings on 2 April 1988, the date of my second photographic excursion to Newington. I had previously pictured Stone Farm intact on 27 February 1988, before it became another victim of the change to the access route. Newington church is just visible beyond the freshly excavated earth bank, which had been cut right back to allow for a diversion to the A20.

Then: This Robert Kennelly study is of Pound Farm's herd of Ayrshire cows being taken to Home Farm for milking. They were introduced by Charles Vincent who had recently taken over from his father Samuel. Miss Marchant said the cows were not supposed to stray onto the grass verges on either side of The Street, although this was easier said than done! The huge Ash tree behind the cows partially conceals the outbuildings of Pound Farm. The building furthest from the camera is the Village Hut, the precursor to today's more substantial village hall.

Now. The War Memorial, which had long since replaced the village pump, is the only unchanged feature in this 1998 view. Far left, the Old Tithe Barn is now completely roofless. In 1977, villagers had complained to a local paper that its Kent-Peg tiles had been removed. Ironically, this prompted the owner to dismantle the barn's 350 year-old rafters as well! To the right, Pound Farm is no more, replaced by a terrace of 1960s style houses.

Then: A 1930s picture of The Street that chronologically fits neatly between the two views featured on p23. The rendered cottages seen earlier, are far left. Standing outside the village shop are Mr and Mrs Easton, he was also the postmaster. To the right of them is a brick fronted cottage, the home of the Smith family. At this time, the Smallest Wealden was occupied by Mrs Toms and her 'deaf and dumb' daughter Lucy. They took in washing to make ends meet. At the far end is the Barley Mow.

Now. A much changed scene today. The Barley Mow is long closed. It was not a public house in the strictest sense, but a beer house or jug room, where drinks had to be taken outside. It was run by Mr Fisher and later, Mr Mardle. The local store and post office closed in October 1965, the last proprietor being Mr Lincoln. Then in 1967, the Smallest Wealden and everything to the left of it was demolished, to be replaced by the buildings we see now.

Then: No. 7 The Street, or Smallest Wealden, in the 1930s. Featured in this view are the former central hall section (left) and the narrow north wing, distinguished by the higher jetty, to the right. The south wing; which was to the left, was clad in brick and geometric tiles and then incorporated into the adjacent house. When the Edwardian properties were constructed to the right of the Smallest Wealden, part of the north wing was cut off to accommodate them. This lost the roof's hipped end, the cat slide at first floor level and reduced the width of the ground floor.

Now. The present property, constructed following demolition of the Smallest Wealden in 1967. The old house received other alterations when its Edwardian neighbours were built, including the insertion of the gabled dormer and through passage in the north wing. Because a section of the north wing had been taken down, a new end wall was constructed, becoming the party wall with the Edwardian development. When the Smallest Wealden perished, this wall remained and can be seen today, preserved between the modern and Edwardian properties.

Three
The Newington Hit List

The old Water Mill at Frogholt on 23 August 1898 when it was still in operation and part of Stockwell's Farm. The mill itself is the timber framed and gabled section (far left), which housed the mechanism, including mill stones and an external water powered mill wheel at the back. The complex was extended in the early nineteenth century, to include the brick built main house, the detached stable block, a paved yard and small bridge over the Seabrook Stream.

The brick built and white painted Mill House, January 1906. The site was mentioned in the Domesday Book and, although no trace of a Norman mill was found here it is possible that one existed nearby as early medieval pottery, recovered locally, would suggest. It is described as a flour mill in a local history book of 1790 and continued as such until 1907, when construction of the new Ashford Road necessitated the diversion of the Seabrook Stream.

The rear of the old mill in the early 1900s during the last years of operation. The water wheel itself is just out of the picture to the right. What can clearly be seen is the mill Stream or race, which provided the actual power. It rejoined the Seabrook Stream proper, just south of the mill. The new Ashford Road was positioned on an embankment a few yards beyond the mill. The Seabrook Stream was then piped beneath the new road and the mill race was filled in.

Mill House in the summer of 1987, during a structural and archaeological investigation. Its splendid external condition can be credited to former owner, Barry Pattinson, who purchased the property in 1977 and is claimed to have spent around £50,000 on renovation work since then. Sadly, it would all be in vain. When Eurotunnel first submitted proposals for building the terminal, Mill House was completely unaffected. However, Shepway District Council were not happy with plans for the access roads; which had serious repercussions for Mill House.

The rear of the mainly nineteenth-century section of Mill House, also from summer 1987. At this time, Eurotunnel's plans included site access roads which left the M20 at Beachborough, then passed to the north of Frogholt and entered (and exited) the terminal area between Newington and Peene. Shepway District Council were concerned that this northern access road would significantly discourage incoming visitors from going to Dover, Folkestone or Hythe. Instead, they proposed an alternative route that would plough straight through Mill House and three other significant properties.

The Mill House stable block, photographed as part of the site investigations which began in summer 1987. With so much to lose, Barry Pattinson, together with other owners affected by 'The Shepway Alternative', decided to protest bitterly against the proposed developments. They had encouraging news when, in November 1986, the Commons Channel Tunnel Select Committee rejected Shepway District Council's proposals. However, the Council, backed by the residents of Newington and Peene, threatened a policy of non co-operation with Eurotunnel if their plans were not accepted. This did the trick and by January 1987, the southern access route was a reality.

Members of the Canterbury Archaeological Trust excavate the foundations of an outbuilding immediately north of Mill House. In May 1987, Shepway District Council formally gave the go-ahead to demolish all buildings in the path of the southern access route, dubbed by the press as 'The Newington Hit List'. The trust began their work shortly afterwards. Sadly, any evidence of an earlier mill here was not found. However, they did manage to re-trace and record the route of the long filled-in mill race.

The eighteenth-century timber-framed section of the former mill being carefully dismantled by the Canterbury Archaeological Trust in March 1988. Eurotunnel agreed to finance the dismantling (and later re-erection) of any historical building significantly affected by their works, which included the earliest part of Mill House. However, during this process it became apparent that due to recent alterations to the structure, its re-erection may not be feasible. To make matters worse, less than a month later, all the Kent-Peg tiles taken into storage by Eurotunnel, were reported as stolen.

The stable block, with demolition in progress, during March 1988. None of the structures from the early nineteenth century phase of construction were deemed worth saving and all met a fate similar to the stable. Behind it is the embankment carrying the part of the Ashford Road constructed in 1907. Before this date, the main road followed a narrow and tortuous route right through the tiny village of Frogholt.

The little brick bridge that once carried horse drawn vehicles, over the Seabrook Stream, to and from the old water mill. The parapets have gone and the structure has cracked under the weight of the demolition machinery. Beyond and to the right, is the mouth of the culvert in the 1907 embankment, through which the Seabrook Stream passes. To the left is the end wall of the partially demolished stable block.

The unsalvaged portion of Mill House being demolished in the spring of 1988. The last remaining fragment (left) is the side porch and back wall of the eighteenth century part of the structure, much of which had been dismantled and stored at that time. Amongst the rubble is a length of decorative chimney and several leaded window frames. Once the debris was cleared away, archaeologists dug beneath for traces of the Domesday mill, but found nothing.

Then: The entire Mill House complex, as seen from just off the A20 in the summer of 1987. There have been remarkably few changes in the external appearance over the years. Sadly though, just another year hence saw not only all the buildings gone, but also all the trees felled. The grounded boat in the foreground remained in place for some months after the Mill House and its surroundings had disappeared.

Now. A bland scene that would not have been photographed were it not the site of the lost Mill House. After the area was cleared in 1988, most of the Seabrook Stream was piped underground and the vast majority of the valley filled in. This was in order to provide an embankment, parallel to the M20, to support the main access road for the terminal. Today, motorway traffic simply filters onto this road, whereas local traffic travels westwards via the A20 at Beachborough, before taking a curving left turn onto it.

Stone Farm was the subject of an imaginative study by Canterbury Archaeological Trust artist, John Bowen. This is the second building on the Newington Hit List. The drawing captures a moment sometime in the eighteenth century, when the farmhouse was extensively re-built. It is closely based on a detailed architectural survey of the structure, undertaken by the trust in 1987. The artwork was commissioned by Eurotunnel and displayed for a number of years in their Visitor Centre. Depicted behind, is the post rider galloping towards Folkestone with the mail.

A romantic view of the creeper clad south wing of Stone Farm by Robert Kennelly in the late 1920s. The building seems all but swamped in vegetation. At this time, Stone Farm was occupied by Mr Buckwell. He was a son of the Rector of Newington, who resided in The Vicarage opposite, another hit-listed property. Stone Farm was a small independent concern unconnected to the big empires run by the Brockmans of Beachborough or Vincents of Pound Farm. It was mainly arable with just a few calves and some poultry.

A slightly later Kennelly study of Stone Farm after much of the adhering greenery had been removed. It gives us a chance to study the rear of this fascinating building. The main part of Stone Farm, built in the mid-sixteenth century, consisted of stone rubble ground floor walls, a timber framed and jettied first floor (except at the rear) and hipped roof. The house was extensively re-ordered and the roof re-built in the eighteenth century. The south wing (right) was also completely replaced at the same time.

Another view from the same spot taken during the trust's study of Stone Farm from Summer 1987 to Spring 1988. With the intervening tree gone, the scene is now uninterrupted. Changes since the 1930s include the blocking up of one ground floor window and the reduction in size of another. Moreover, the eighteenth century timber framed south wing has been completely replaced by a modern brick extension. Encompassed within the raised patio area, in the angle between main house and wing, is a deep brick-lined well.

The east end of Stone Farm from the side track, where begins a footpath to Hythe. The Canterbury Archaeological Trust's architectural survey was authorized once it was clear that, like Mill House, Stone Farm was in the path of the new southern road access route. Original plans had always included southern rail access, with lines passing to the east of Stone Farm, then crossing over the A20 before entering the terminal. The revised plans meant that now, entrance and exit road bridges crossed the A20 alongside the rail bridge.

The north side of the doomed Stone Farm from across the A20. The compromise reached between Eurotunnel and Shepway in January 1987, known as 'The Joint Southern Access' (i.e. road and rail), called for three bridges over the A20, with the two road bridges required to be west of the rail bridge. Stone Farm was clearly in the way. As with Mill House, the owners had spent both time and money on renovation work. However, unlike other owners, they did not court publicity, despite being forced to quit their home.

Outbuildings belonging to Stone Farm in the last few months, prior to the site being levelled. As was the case with Pound Farm, Stone Farm was the name of both the farmhouse and farm. The barn continued to be in use right up to its compulsory purchase by Eurotunnel. In the foreground is one of the Canterbury Archaeological Trust's trenches. Their investigations revealed traces of a house and outbuildings from the fourteenth century, that preceded the sixteenth century Stone Farm development.

Another view from the farmyard, this one looks north across the A20 and into Newington. By now, many of the outbuildings were in a somewhat run down condition and some were without a roof. On the opposite side of the main road is the Police House standing at the junction for The Street, Newington. Further right and atop the bank is a grounded railway wagon, standing in what was a narrow pasture to the west of the Glebe Field.

The exposed rafters of Stone Farm in March 1988. It was always thought that Stone Farm was a candidate for dismantling rather than demolition, a fact confirmed during the Canterbury Archaeological Trust's meticulous architectural survey of the structure. Most of the roof timbers dated from the eighteenth century re-building of the farm. Only the hipped roof members at the east end (right) were from the original construction period of the mid-sixteenth century. Visible beyond is the bungalow Lone Pine, to where the Philpotts had recently moved from Danton Lane Cottages.

The front (north) elevation of the house from the A20. Note the front door propped up against the scaffolding. With the roof now gone, the dismantling team began work on the sixteenth century timbers of the upper storey. For many years, the first floor timber frame had been hidden externally by hung tiles and these were the first things to be removed. Throughout this process, each item was carefully photographed, documented and numbered, which would greatly help when re-assembling the frames, whenever or wherever this was to happen.

40

The ground floor stone rubble walls of Stone Farm, standing stripped of all salvageable components. It is now possible to look beyond both north and south window apertures to the M20 beyond. The dismantling of the timber frame was very rapid, taking less than a month to complete. Everything was then taken into secure storage at Ashford, where it would remain for some years. All that remained was for the unwanted parts of Stone Farm to be pulled down.

Demolition in progress at Stone Farm during the last week of March 1988. A wall of the south wing visibly buckles before the excavator. Debris from the four hundred-year-old stone rubble walls is strewn all around. Shortly after this, work began on the three bridges for the A20 and the two required to span the M20.

Then: Stone Farm in 1986 in happier times surrounded by the fresh green foliage of early summer. In July of the same year, local papers first reported that the House of Commons Select Committee had agreed to investigate an alternative access route proposed by Shepway District Council. The nightmare for residents on the Newington Hit List then began.

Now. The grey, grim pillars of the A20 bridges, over which thousands travel by road and rail, to and from the Channel Tunnel Terminal on a daily basis. How many people are aware that as they cross, beneath them lies a site where, for hundreds of years, a family home and working farm enjoyed a peaceful and uninterrupted existence? After its removal, nothing more was heard about Stone Farm until 1995, when the timbers were sold by auction and subsequently re-erected as part of a house in Sandling Road, Saltwood near Hythe.

Then: Single storey cattle sheds, part of the complex of outbuildings at Stone Farm that could be seen whilst waiting for a Hythe bound bus from Newington. Behind and to the right, is the side wall of Forge Cottage. Having levelled the remains of Stone Farm, the excavator progressed onto the outbuildings and made short work of their destruction.

Now. A gentle grass-covered embankment is all that can be seen from the bus stop today. Beyond the fence is the main incoming access road for the terminal, which has run parallel to the M20 since Beachborough. It crosses the first of the three bridges over the A20 immediately to the left. The middle bridge carries out-going road traffic, which has to cross over the M20, in order to exit at Beachborough on the south side of the motorway.

A garden party taking place in the grounds of Newington Vicarage, probably in the last quarter of the nineteenth century. The presence of many Union Flags suggests the celebration of a royal occasion, perhaps Queen Victoria's Golden Jubilee of 1887, or Diamond Jubilee of 1897. Behind can be seen the creeper covered west elevation of Newington Vicarage itself. This impressive eight bedroom house was built in 1868 to replace the property just off The Street; which thereafter became known as The Old Vicarage.

The south elevation of Newington Vicarage, drawn by R.L. Buckwell in about 1920. The driveway led to the south side of the house where the front door was situated, but the actual 'front' of the house was the grander west elevation. The artist was probably one of the Revd Leyton Buckwell's ten children. Revd Buckwell was Rector of Newington from 1880 to 1920. The incumbent was dependent for his living on the Brockmans, owners of the Beachborough Estate. Mr Brockman was once heard to remark that this family had nearly ruined him!

The east side of Newington Vicarage, also drawn by R.L. Buckwell during the family's residency. As is usual with the 'back' of a large house, this is where the domestic offices could be found. The next occupant was Revd Frederick John Picard, who remained until 1932, when Newington became a joint living with Cheriton and the vicarage put up for sale by auction. The catalogue describes it as a 'freehold country residence' complete with outbuildings, including stables that encompass a coach house. Once sold, the house became Newington Grange.

The north elevation of Newington Grange can be seen from between the trees lining The Grove, during the mid-1980s. By this time, many changes had taken place, most notably, the splitting up of the original two acre grounds into three separate plots. The most northerly third now belonged to a postwar house called Skarthi and it is the lawn of this house that we look across in this view. The remaining grounds were split between Newington Grange, now divided into flats, and the original detached Coach House which had been converted into a dwelling.

The front, or south side, of the Coach House in 1986, after it had become a private residence. Built in 1868, at the same time as the main house, it is described in the 1932 sale catalogue as a 'range of stabling containing coach house, harness room with fireplace, two stall stable with loose box, wash house and large living room over'. In 1986 it was owned by Tony and Christine Fry. The Frys were in the middle of a renovation programme; which had cost £20,000 at that time.

The western end of the Coach House that overlooked the former domestic offices of Newington Grange. For local residents, the first tangible evidence that the Channel Tunnel scheme was more than a bad dream, appeared in April 1986. Notices were put up all over Newington, giving advance warning of the diversion or closure of any roads, bridle ways or footpaths affected by the forthcoming works. At this stage, the only village houses affected were Newington Grange and The Coach House.

The north elevation of the Coach House, with Pine trees bordering The Grove visible behind. In April 1986, the Frys learned that their driveway, and only vehicular access onto the A20 (i.e. The Grove), would be blocked by a new railway embankment giving access to the terminal. However, this issue paled in comparison with the acceptance of the Joint Southern Access scheme in January 1987, when the Grange and Coach House were added to the Newington Hit List.

Glebe Field in the late summer sunshine of 1987 with linear archaeology trenches crossing the area. Beyond the hedge to the right is the A20, with Newington Grange and Coach House hidden by vegetation to the left. In the distance is The Grove, with Vicarage Meadow beyond. The Joint Southern Access meant that the original plans for a narrow railway embankment bisecting this area, was now replaced by a much wider elevated approach, carrying both road and rail, eliminating it completely.

The grandest of Newington Grange's elevations, the west side, during a break in demolition, probably around Christmas 1987. This house was the first to go as a result of the Channel Tunnel scheme. Neither Newington Grange nor Coach House were listed properties and thus were never considered for dismantling. The Joint Southern Access scheme proved to be very destructive. Ironically, the scheme had been enthusiastically supported by most Newington residents; who were unhappy that the original northern access roads divided them from Peene. Peene and Newington were two villages; but were locally considered as one community.

Part of the south side of the Grange, including the front door, with demolition in progress. Right, are the original library windows, with bedroom (right) and dressing room windows (left) above. The agreement and implementation of the Joint Southern Access plan caused bad feelings between Newington residents and the owners of properties on the hit list who were, after all, residents of Newington. There was also genuine shock at the amount of demolition needed to implement a scheme they had supported in good faith.

An interesting study showing the relationship between the Coach House and the, by now gutted, Newington Grange. The single storey and gable-ended east wing of the main house, once contained the kitchen and scullery. The Victorian Society had protested against the planned demolition, describing the buildings as 'forming a good group comprising of vicarage and coach house which are a rare survival in their well preserved state for this area'. Sadly, these words were drowned out by the noise of the demolition machines.

A section of Newington Grange's northern elevation in its last moments. During the vicarage days, the ground floor windows lit (left to right) the butlers pantry, main WC and cloakroom. On the first floor is the bathroom (left) and north bedroom (right) with attic bedroom above. The basement which housed a larder, wine and beer cellars, was beneath this section of the house. Demolition had resumed by the second week of January 1988 and was soon completed. The basement was filled with demolition material, a gem to be re-discovered by future archaeologists.

Then: Newington Vicarage, as it was then, at the beginning of the twentieth century, when the incumbent was the Revd Buckwell. The grand west side of the house was also where the principal rooms could be found. Behind the embayed window (right) is the drawing room, the dining room is on the left and the garden door in the middle. On the first floor are the windows of the main bedrooms, the one on the right had a connecting dressing room.

Now. Part of the Elham Valley Way, which now passes between Newington and the Channel Tunnel Terminal. The A20 is to the right and Lone Pine to the left. This position is slightly further back than that of the *then* picture, which is now occupied by the broad access embankment. Lifelong Newington resident, Miss Marchant, feels that if both northern and southern road access schemes had been presented together, with all the implications spelt out, then the results could have been very different. Perhaps Newington Grange would be standing today.

Four

Peene

The tiny village of Peene, from the Elham Valley Railway embankment, by Robert Kennelly in the early 1930s. Most of the village is visible here, situated on a gentle slope, which becomes more severe on the approach to the Cheriton Downs. Its Old English name *pund* means pound or enclosure and the hamlet probably developed around a farm situated on one of the Seabrook Stream tributaries. By 1304, the name was recorded as *Pende*, then spelt *Pean* as recently as on the 1937 Ordnance Survey map.

The south side of the farmhouse to Peene Bridge Farm, with its glorious cottage garden, in the 1930s. The small farm was run by the Vincents, who also let out this cottage. It probably dates from the late seventeenth century, although the roof's steep pitch may indicate the existence of an earlier timber frame hidden beneath later work. In any case, there is clear evidence of subsidence in the cracked and undulating brickwork. Strengthening iron tie-bars have also been installed above the ground floor windows.

Rose Cottages (left), situated just after a tight bend around Peene Bridge Farm. In the early 1930s, these long narrow single storey dwellings were occupied by two large families. Further along the lane is the steep sloping roof of Peene House. Rose Cottages did not survive much beyond the date of this picture. After demolition, planning permission was sought for a replacement house to accommodate the Peene House gardener. Permission was never granted and the plot later sold. Eventually, a modern bungalow appeared on the site.

The front of Peene House in the early 1930s, probably on a day in June, a month when the old rambling roses are at their best. The occupant at this time was Miss Violet Weall. Peene House is an early example of a timber frame Wealden type hall, albeit much altered over the years. Historian E.W. Larkin asserts that the heavy timbers of its *sans-purlin* roof, suggest that it was built in the first half of the fourteenth century.

More climbing roses adorn Nos 1 & 2 Peene House Cottages, another Kennelly study. They were formerly known as Pebble Cottages, because of their unusual pebble facing. Both houses were owned by the Brockmans, who let them out. At this time, one of the cottages was occupied by the Crouchers, who were jobbing gardeners.

A 1930s view of Peene that has changed very little today. On the left are Peene House Cottages and to the right, the first of five rendered dwellings called Peene Cottages. Further up the slope is a terrace of six more recent houses, also called Peene Cottages. The farm track serves the upper houses and fields beyond, known as Whitelands Fields and owned by the Brockmans. Just to the right of the track is a gully, through which a seasonal brook flows.

Nos 1 to 5 Peene Cottages, with their long front gardens dedicated to cottage flowers. The vegetables were grown in the back gardens. No. 5 (furthest right) is the home of Harry and Emily Amos and the place where Robert Kennelly lodged during his summer visits to the area. Engineer and builder Harry Amos, was known locally as 'Spratt' to distinguish him from the many other people named Amos in the area. He retired at the age of seventy-three, just after the Second World War.

54

Faced back onto Peene from just off Hill Lane. To the left is the rear of No. 5 Peene Cottages, the home of the Amoses. Both Harry and Emily were well-known village characters. He used to make his own wine and process his own tobacco. In 1959, when Mr Amos was eighty-five, they celebrated their golden wedding anniversary. Both spent the rest of their lives at No. 5, Harry died there in 1973, just six months short of his 100th birthday.

Another view facing down onto Peene, but further back from Whitelands Fields, so as to include both rows of Peene Cottages. The electricity pylons are a recent addition to the landscape which were erected in about 1930. Rachel Marchant remembers being taken to hear the wind whistle through them. A view from the same vantage point today may include Underhill Cottages to the left. These were built by the local council immediately before and just after the Second World War.

The ploughed and harrowed fields above Peene in the winter of 1987. Peene itself is to the right, with Underhill Cottages prominent. The worked fields in the foreground are safe, but those in the middle distance and beyond, will soon become the site for the Channel Tunnel Terminal. Linear archaeological trenches which cut across this area can just be made out. In the distance is the long tree covered embankment of the former Elham Valley Railway.

An archaeological investigation in 1988. It is situated at the northerly edge of the vast area, by then already cleared for the terminal. Underhill Cottages at Peene are in the middle distance (left) with the site of Peene Bridge Farm just off camera to the left. The dig found evidence that a Roman settlement had existed here. Pottery relating to the period and also the early Bronze Age was recovered.

Then: A busy late summers day haymaking at Peene Bridge Farm in the early 1930s. A cart has just emptied its load into the yard beyond (left) whilst another, laden with hay, waits to do the same. No doubt, the Vincent's head waggoner Jack Heyman, is overseeing the proceedings. Peene Bridge Farm had recently been absorbed by the Vincent family, despite the fact it did not have much land of its own. The farmhouse, to the right, would soon fall into disrepair and ultimately be demolished.

Now. The same site today, now the home for Peene Railway Museum, dedicated to the memory of the Elham Valley Line. The abutments to Peene Bridge and a short length of surviving railway embankment can be found next to the museum. The complex includes a 250 year-old barn that once stood at Danton Farm. Donated by Eurotunnel to the Elham Valley Line Trust, it was re-erected here after a short period in store.

Then: A charming Robert Kennelly study of the east end of Peene House from the 1930s. Once again an old rose, possibly the rambler *Albertine*, beautifies the facade. Although much older, Peene House was similar in construction to Stone Farm, in having stone rubble ground floor walls, with a timber framed upper-storey and roof, all later completely faced in tiles. The main difference was that Peene House, as originally built, had an open central hall (as did Pound Farm).

Now: The east end of Peene House in 1998, during renovation work. Long after Miss Weall's time, the house was sub-divided into flats. It was acquired by Eurotunnel, who in 1987, invited enquiries from licensees about the possibility of Peene House becoming a public house. This fell through as nobody seemed to want a pub in Peene! The recent renovation included the under-pinning and shoring up of the subsiding south-east corner. During this remedial work, it was discovered that Peene House had no foundations whatsoever.

Five
The Elham Valley Line

New railway wagons, out-shopped from Ashford Works, being stored on the closed Elham Valley Line just west of Peene Bridge in 1952. Trains had ceased to run in 1947 and much of the line was lifted. However, the section from Cheriton Junction to Eachendhill was retained for wagon storage until 1953, when the remaining track was taken up.

Peene Bridge being dismantled and cut up on site in 1967, having seen its last train, albeit for the track lifting gang, in 1953. Many of the former line's metal bridges were taken down around this time, as they could be subject to deterioration and become unsafe. Brick arches and bridges were left intact, as were the brick buttresses to Peene Bridge, which can still be seen today in excellent condition.

The first of two occupation arches in the embankment east of Peene Bridge, from the south side. These arches were usually provided over rights of way, or as in this case, to allow farmers access to their fields on either side of the line. The story of the Elham Valley Line actually began at Peene, where the first sod was cut, amidst much official clamour, on 28 August 1884. Brick arches and bridges along this part of the line were built in 1885.

The second and most easterly occupation arch, facing towards Newington, in February 1988. This spanned a well-used footpath from Danton Pinch. During construction of the line Newington residents lobbied for a station to be built here; but this came to nothing. Instead, local passengers had to board and alight at Cheriton. One of them was William Marchant who travelled weekly to the Corn Exchange at Canterbury. The Marchant sisters would run to wave at him as the train passed over Peene Bridge.

A view from Star Bridge on the A20, looking along the empty trackbed towards Peene as shown in this 1965 photograph by the fifteen year-old Brian Hart. The shallow cutting beneath the bridge soon levelled out before the line mounted the long embankment towards Peene. The embankment is made from chalk spoil, excavated from the deep cutting at Eachendhill, further up the line. The result of all the earthworks was a line with a steady 1:90 gradient climb from Cheriton to Eachendhill.

Another Brian Hart picture, this one of Star Bridge itself from the empty trackbed and looking down the overgrown cutting towards Cheriton Junction. This robust, yet attractive bridge, of reinforced concrete with Kentish ragstone parapets, replaced the original brick bridge in 1932, when the A20 was created. Officially called Newington Bridge, it was usually referred to by locals as Star Bridge after the adjacent pub on the A20.

Cheriton Junction from the main line, by Brian Hart, in 1965. The long abandoned and overgrown cutting of the Elham Valley Line curves away to the right. Star Bridge crossed the cutting a few hundred yards beyond. By 1989, it contained many mature trees and had become a real haven for wildlife. To the dismay of the local people, in May of that year, the trees were felled and the cutting bulldozed. Eventually in 1992, Eurotunnel erected their new administration building across the filled in cutting.

Star Bridge looking south, at the beginning of demolition, in mid March 1966. Reputedly, it was being removed to eliminate a traffic danger spot. In this photograph the ragstone parapets have gone. This would prove to be the easy part of the demolition. Later that month, the bridge's northern span resisted two attempts of demolition by dynamite. It then had to be halved with pneumatic drills. The southern span was similarly despatched in early April. At that time, demolition contractors commented that the bridge had been made too strong!

The second occupation arch looking south, shown here during demolition in mid 1988. The parapets have already gone and trees on either side are in the process of being grubbed up. These arches were used extensively by the local farmers over the years, especially the Vincents, and had become a familiar part of the landscape. However, Miss Marchant well remembers the large impassable puddles that would form under them every winter!

A bulldozer topples mature trees at the eastern end of the railway embankment at Peene in summer 1988. Many oaks had seeded onto the vacant trackbed which, after thirty-five years of undisturbed growth, had become a linear woodland supporting all forms of wildlife. Once the trees had been despatched, massive grading machines moved in to level the old embankment. During this process, the embankment's white chalk core was exposed for the first time since construction in 1885.

Facing west onto the truncated remains of the railway embankment in the autumn of 1988. Approximately 100 yards of embankment still existed at Peene and ended abruptly at the edge of the terminal site. In the foreground, Canterbury Archaeological Trust uncover traces of pre-medieval settlements. In 1989, a huge earth bank, or *bund*, was erected around the perimeter of the terminal, shielding local residents from the sight and sound of construction. The remains of the embankment were joined onto this *bund*.

Then: The east occupation arch facing Danton Pinch; which is just visible beyond and which provided the inspiration for me to start this whole project. The Elham Valley Line, opened in 1887, had been built to mainline standards with gentle curves and gradients, as well as a double track throughout. It is sad to reflect that such a well-built railway would only last for sixty years.

Now. The duty-free building and associated parking in 1998, on the exact spot where the Elham Valley Line once crossed the Danton Pinch footpath. The high-speed rail link is currently (during 2001) being built to exacting standards. Similar care was given to constructing the Elham Valley Line. This meant cuttings, embankments and occupation arches, instead of the steeper gradients and level crossings of a light railway. Had the line remained open, it would have provided direct rail access to the terminal and tunnel beyond. Imagine, Eurostars speeding over Peene Bridge!

Then: Star Bridge looking north towards Peene in 1965. The cutting it spans was one of the first earthworks undertaken in the line's construction. The South East Railways chairman, Sir Edward Watkin, was the driving force behind the building of the Elham Valley Railway. One of his other passions was the construction of a Channel Tunnel. The line would have played an important part in his dream to link England with mainland Europe. It is ironic that his railway should cross an area ultimately chosen for the Channel Tunnel Terminal.

Now. Facing north across the M20 and along the route of the disappeared railway. After Star Bridge had been demolished, that part of the cutting was filled in and the A20 relaid on top. Then, between 1976 and 1981, the M20 extension to Folkestone was built. The new motorway took over the route of the A20 at this location, so the A-road was re-aligned further north. Finally, in 1988 construction of the terminal wiped out all remaining traces of the former Elham Valley Line to just short of Peene.

Six

Danton Pinch

Cousins James Hinchcliffe, James Moorhouse and Ellen Cotton relax in the front garden of *Its-It*, Danton Pinch, in the 1930s. Danton Pinch was a speculative scheme of nine building plots arranged along a footpath below the Cheriton Hills. It was positioned just east of Beargarden Woods, at a point where the path from Peene, half a mile to the west, met the path up from Newington. The scheme was conceived in about 1920 by landowner Martin Henry. Lombardy Poplars were planted to mark the boundaries of each plot, which were then offered for sale.

Plots 5 to 7 Danton Pinch, following purchase by the Moorhouses in 1922 for £100. The price included a partially erected bungalow on plot 5 (right), later named *Its-It*. This property was made up from two second-hand army huts fixed together at right angles. Also visible is an old bus body, used as a shed, and a summer house on a turntable, so that it could be made to face the sun. The Moorhouses also grazed sheep on their two non-residential plots.

Young Brian Ivory and his friends, pose around a wigwam in the front garden of *Treetops* (plot 4) in the late 1930s. Beyond the garden fence and left is No. 3a, part of a large impressive house. Further east is the roof and chimney of Eastgate (plot 1). A number of the Poplar trees, planted on the original boundary lines are also featured. Furthest right is the roof of the cottage that preceded The Danes in Danton Lane.

Mrs Moorhouse, wearing a floral dress, with Carrie and Alfred, in the front garden of *Its-It* during 1952. Her bungalow is not visible, but *Treetops* next door and No. 3a are. After Mrs Moorhouse lost her husband in 1950, her niece May and great nephew David Oakley moved in to look after her. They continued to live there after she died, aged ninety, in the 1960s.

Sally Ivory, wearing the uniform of the 3rd Cheriton Girl Guides, in the front garden at *Treetops* in about 1955. As with other families, the Ivorys kept pets over the years. A favourite from this decade was a tame jackdaw called Jeff. The bird would steal items from other households, including jewellery, and eat window putty. Jeff also used to terrorize Mrs Moorhouse next door. However, one day inside *Its-It*, she pulled a feather out of his tail and he never bothered her again.

The frontage of *Cliff End* (plot 9) in February 1969, at the westernmost end of Danton Pinch. The Tyrells had brought *Cliff End* from Mr and Mrs Humphries in 1966, for £3,300. Their daughter Wendy was born there in 1968, delivered by district nurse, Miss Rachel Marchant. In 1969, the property was bought by the Department of the Environment for £6,000, in advance of the earlier Channel Tunnel scheme. Heather Tyrell stayed on as a short-term tenant until moving out on 'decimalisation day' in 1971.

A small bridge and style mark the starting point of a once well-trodden footpath from Danton Pinch to Newington. This was taken by Sally Elwood (née Ivory), during a nostalgic final visit in early 1988. No doubt she recalled those wintry walks across this field to Newington School in the early 1950s. She would skirt the edge of Beargarden Woods before passing through the railway occupation arch and on to School Lane. The wood had long since gone, but the arch can still be seen in the distance.

Cliff End on 27 February 1988, boarded up and awaiting demolition. The earlier government backed tunnel scheme was finally cancelled on the grounds of cost in 1975. However, *Cliff End* was not sold, but continued to be rented out until eventually being passed on to Eurotunnel in 1987. Before the tunnel, the only threat to *Cliff End* came in 1944, when it was occupied by the Mayott family. A doodlebug landed in a nearby field and blew away part of the house front, which had to be shored up.

Braewood (plot 8) in February 1988, the next property in this sequential batch of more recent pictures. Plot 8 had always been owned by the adjacent *Cliff End* and for many years, a large shed stood at the back of the area. Then in 1966, *Cliff End* owners, the Humphries, built *Braewood* for themselves and sold *Cliff End* to the Tyrells. The last occupants, the Seymours, reluctantly moved out a week before the hurricane of 16 October 1987. On that stormy night, a tree crashed through their old bedroom at *Braewood*.

Facing east along Danton Pinch, in early 1988, towards Sally Elwood's car, parked outside her old home *Treetops*. Left, are the hedges concealing *Braewood* and the large plot associated with *Its-It*. There has been surprisingly little speculation as to why Danton Pinch was so-named. Mrs Moorhouse used to insist that it was because horses' collars would pinch as they rounded the corner onto the cul-de-sac. Another explanation offered was that the lane itself gradually 'pinched' down to almost nothing.

A panoramic view of the *Its-It* small holding, looking east, in the mid 1960s. It was taken from the roof of the large shed at the rear of plot 8, reputed to have been the oldest building at Canton Pinch. Mr Humphries was to demolish this structure, ably assisted by David Oakley and his cousin Tom, to free the site for *Braewood*.

The curiously named *Its-It* from the long front garden in August 1963. Provision of mains water supply was still a few years away, so in the meantime, residents continued to collect and boil rain water. Original owners, the Moorhouses, always intended to replace this temporary structure with a brick built bungalow. However, ill health and the Second World War prevented this. Postwar resident, May Oakley, talked about the coming of the Channel Tunnel as far back as the 1950s, so rebuilding of *Its-It* never seemed practical!

Keen gardener, May Oakley, shows off her roses in front of *Its-It* in 1972. She and her son David, remained freeholders until finally being forced to sell to Eurotunnel in 1987. *Treetops* next door, was built in the 1920s by northerner Walter Jarman, who had moved south after contracting tuberculosis. The bungalow's original name was *Trevorlawn*, after Walter's son. The property was purchased by David and Queenie Ivory in 1933-1934 and it was Queenie who changed the name to *Treetops*.

Facing west in early 1988, towards *Cliff End*. All the other properties were set well back in a straight line. Tom Oakley speculated that when first built, Danton Pinch consisted of two parallel roads, an upper one for direct access to the houses and a lower road for tradesmen. Presumably, the one seen here was the original wider lower road and that an upper access path immediately in front of the set-back houses fell out of use very early on.

Treetops as re-discovered by Sally Elwood in early 1988. Her former childhood home was now boarded up and there was no trace of the massive grapevine that once grew in the front conservatory. The Ivorys temporarily moved out of *Treetops* during the Second World War, because of its vulnerable position perched high up on the downs. Sally was born at Sandgate whilst they were away. On returning, the Ivorys spent many happy years at *Treetops*, making improvements, including the installation of dormer windows in the 1950s.

The asymmetrical and nameless semi-detached houses, Nos 3 (right) and 3a (left) Danton Pinch, on 27 February 1988. Despite the Edwardian appearance, they were built in the 1920s, originally to be one house. Plot 3 was bought by a man, who started to build a house as a wedding present for his daughter. Sadly, before it was finished, the wedding was called off. The house stood as an empty, incomplete shell for about ten years and when finally finished, emerged as two uneven semi-detached houses.

The bungalow *Downside* (plot 2), with its impressive wrap-around conservatory, in February 1988. Previous occupants include the Cossalls and the Buckleys, who ran a chemist's shop in Guildhall Street, Folkestone. Their daughter Jackie was a good friend of Sally Ivory from *Treetops*. *Downside* was one of the Danton Pinch properties bought up in the late 1960s, prior to the earlier government backed attempt to build a Channel Tunnel. The last to rent were Charles and Anne Taperell.

The charming house *Eastgate*, amidst the mature trees on its three quarter acre plot, in February 1988. This property was the easternmost in Danton Pinch and stood near the junction with Danton Lane. The original owners were the Wards, who later rented the property to Howard Phillp. The Alexanders lived at *Eastgate* for many years. They were keen gardeners and planted the trees visible here. Final occupants were newly weds Phyllis and Arthur Bone, who took residence in 1968.

The site of *Eastgate* from the same position in September 1988. Little remains of this once immaculate pink painted house, except a small pile of rubble that had been missed by the passing land graders. Behind, redundant electricity and telegraph poles still stand in the severed stump of Danton Lane. Danton Pinch had been demolished in April and May that year, except *Cliff End*, which hung on for a short while longer.

A small fragment of Danton Pinch still hanging on in September 1988. These are the in-situ front garden steps of *Eastgate* that once led up to the house from the junction with Danton Lane. Chunks of the demolished house and a few rock plants from the once well-tended garden are also evident. Tom Oakley had visited *The Pinch* earlier during demolition and rescued the curved ribs from inside the old bus body at *Its-It*.

The shattered remains of a subterranean water storage tank, in September 1988, the only other evidence that a community had once existed here. Most Danton Pinch properties had such tanks for the collection of rainwater, in the absence of a mains supply. They measured approximately eleven feet across and were nine feet deep. All became redundant upon the arrival of mains water in about 1966. Danton Pinch also did not have an electricity supply until 1964.

Then: The prominent house *Cliff End* on 27 February 1988, still impressive despite its derelict and boarded up status. It had been built by the man who created Danton Pinch, Martin Henry, who had originally called it *Eastwood*. Mr Henry insisted that all the other properties be built set well back, so as not to obscure the panoramic views from his house! 1960s owner, Heather Tyrell, commented that the property was much smaller within than it first appeared from the outside.

Now. Facing west along the currently empty car and coach customer access route, towards the Control Centre (left) with lorries stacking up on the freight access route to the right. It is hard to imagine that *Cliff End* ever stood here. All the former residents enjoyed their stay, including the last occupants, father and daughter David and Nichola Pollock, who rented *Cliff End* from the Department of the Environment. It was the last Danton Pinch house to be demolished, going in the summer of 1988.

Then: James Hinchcliffe and owner James Moorhouse (right) take tea in the front garden of *Its-It* in the 1930s. Behind is the dormer-less *Trevorlawn*, later to become *Treetops* and beyond, the empty and incomplete shell of No. 3/3a. Danton Pinch was a tightly knit community where everyone was considered equal, in spite of the differing status of the properties. Then, later in the 1960s, when some houses were bought by the government, long-term freeholders happily co-existed with the short-let renters of the Department of the Environment owned dwellings.

Now. The terminal site's access roads looking east in 1998. The arrow on the gantry above indicates that cars are about to stream onto a shuttle train beyond. If you want to enjoy tea at the same spot today, it would have to be whilst on the move. Residents of the lost hamlet endured many hardships together, not least of which was the lack of mains services until the 1960s. Moreover, the threat of the Channel Tunnel throughout the post-war years, was also a shared concern.

Then: Sally Elwood, between her children Matthew and Emma, in the front garden of No. 3a, during their final nostalgic visit in early 1988. Captain Donoghue, last resident of 3a, and of Danton Pinch, was still there at the time. In fact, he left it so late to leave, that the removal van found the south end of Danton Lane already severed. Sally remembered an earlier occupant, Mrs Foad, and the run-ins with her parents concerning the dividing hedge between *Treetops* and No. 3a, which blocked all the light from their kitchen.

Now. The same scene today dominated by the shuttle access roads, with the perimeter service road hidden behind the hedge line. In fact, a much older hedge can still be found at this location today. Beyond the perimeter fence of the terminal, is the original back hedge line of the Danton Pinch properties. Over the years, David Oakley buried three of his beloved pet dogs beneath that rear hawthorn hedge at *Its-It*. Danton Pinch has long gone, but the hedge and pets' graves still exist today.

80

Seven
Along the Main Road

Looking down the Seabrook Valley at Frogholt, from the old Ashford Road, in the early 1900s. The road between Frogholt and Cheriton saw many changes as it adapted to the needs of the motor car. In the early 1930s, it was widened and straightened to become the A20. Between 1976 and 1981, its successor the M20, extended into the area. As a result, the landscape was altered and buildings were lost, that is even before the changes caused by the Channel Tunnel are considered.

Osier Tree Cottage, nestling in the Seabrook Valley south of Frogholt, in the early 1930s. Its relative position to the Ashford Road and Mill House can be ascertained from the previous picture. For many years the cottage was occupied by Mr and Mrs Peter Walter, of Walter & Son shoe shop. Sadly, it was subject to a compulsory purchase order in 1976 and became an early victim of the M20 extension. Moreover, the valley was filled in at this location to support the new motorway.

Facing west along the old Ashford Road, from the junction with The Street, Newington (right) in 1929. The road curves round The Old Forge, a building often frequented by the local farmers. The blacksmith's living quarters are nearest, with the smithy in a single storey projection, at the far (west) end. Far right is the malt house belonging to Home Farm. Both buildings soon became victims of road widening, to create the A20. In fact, some trees to the right had already been felled in preparation.

Another view of The Old Forge, Newington. The overall shape of the building is reminiscent of Stone Farm and the existence of a continuous jetty along the north (street facing) elevation, suggests a similar sixteenth century date and method of construction. By 1930, The Old Forge had become a traffic bottleneck (collision damage is clearly evident) and inevitably, the coming of the A20 would mean its demolition. The New Forge House, behind the tree (left), is being built well back to accommodate the new wider road.

A typical Robert Kennelly study, featuring the west end of Stone Farm almost lost behind the lush summer foliage. Note the two lean-to extensions, the furthest one was a coal and wood store with an access door into the house. The house dates from the sixteenth century and was built from new with a completely enclosed upper storey. This was a progression from the earlier open hall type house, examples of which include Pound Farm and Peene House.

An Edwardian period picture of Newington Vicarage, later Newington Grange, from the north-west. At the time, it was the home to the twelve strong Buckwell family. The Ashford Road is a couple of hundred yards to the right. In fact, the 1932 sale particulars were very precise about the property's situation, describing it as 'about three miles from Folkestone, on the main Folkestone to London Road, about one and a half miles from Shorncliffe Railway Station' and adding 'standing well back from the main road'.

The Ashford Road east of Newington in about 1930. The road narrows as it gently descends, between high-sided grassy banks, towards Stone Farm and The Old Forge. Amidst the pine trees on the right is the junction of the old coaching road, known locally as The Grove. It is also the drive to Newington Vicarage. Vicarage Meadow borders The Grove to the north (right), with Glebe Field to its south.

The new road sign erected at the junction with The Street, on completion of the A20, stage two, from Frogholt to Cheriton in 1932. The new road, made from white concrete sections, is visible beyond the sign. Soil from the roadworks was taken, via temporary light railway, to fill in the course of Scotts Lane, part of which formed the old coaching route from Frogholt, that emerged in Newington as the 'T-Path'. It then continued eastwards along what later became School Lane and The Grove.

A route march along the new wide concrete A20 in about 1932. Having passed Newington, then Longport Farm, the soldiers are now alongside the white rendered public house The Star. Once past the inn, they crossed the newly opened Newington, or Star Bridge, which went over the Elham Valley Line. They then passed by the junction for Danton Lane before approaching Cheriton and possibly going on to Shorncliffe Camp.

An empty Forge Cottage in April 1988, just prior to demolition. As mentioned earlier, it had been constructed in about 1930 to replace The Old Forge, pulled down for road widening. When first built, The New Forge had a decorative parapet, but this had to be removed as it caused the roof to leak. It became Forge Cottage when a local blacksmith was no longer needed. The last residents were Sidney and Florence Shorter. Although doomed by the Joint Southern Access, Forge Cottage was never mentioned alongside other properties on The Newington Hit List.

Stone Farm in its last days, on 27 February 1988. During the next week, the dismantling process began, followed by the demolition of the unwanted parts. Because of its location hard against the A20 at Newington, Stone Farm was the most visible of all the properties doomed by the Channel Tunnel. Other Joint Southern Access 'hit-listed' buildings were largely hidden behind trees and the houses of Danton Lane and Danton Pinch were well off the beaten track.

The clubhouse of Folkestone Rugby Club, on the north side of the A20, in April 1988. They had moved to this seven-acre site, known as Burlington Field, in 1977 once the threat of the previous government backed 'Chunnel' scheme had passed. Behind the clubhouse were two rugby pitches, arranged end to end, which ran parallel to and north of Vicarage Meadow. In February 1986, Eurotunnel asked the club to look for an alternative site, promising compensation and help with the purchase of a new ground.

Longport, the former farmhouse to Longport Farm, situated east of Burlington Field, in the mid 1980s. Longport was never threatened by the Channel Tunnel, falling as it did just outside the development area for the terminal complex. However, the south portal of the loop tunnel, through which every shuttle train would run to turn round, was to be situated immediately north of the house. Ironically, although the owners had been prepared to sell *Longport* to Eurotunnel, they were unable to reach an agreement.

Newington Cricket Ground in 1987, looking northeast from the A20. It was situated between *Longport* and, until recently, the Star Inn. The hexagonal reinforced concrete pillbox, left of the pavilion, is one of the Imperial War Museums 'H- series', also known as a 'type 22', built in 1940 as an anti-invasion defence. The old cricket ground made the headlines in May 1988, when Newington residents complained that it, together with Burlington Field, had become a makeshift caravan site for Channel Tunnel workers.

The beautifully proportioned Star Inn in the 1960s, at a location where the A20 changed from being Ashford Road to Cheriton High Street. Changes since its appearance in the 1930s picture include the revision of its name from The Star to Star Inn, the construction of the 1930s style porches and the elimination of the front bay window. Sadly, the inn was demolished in 1976, when this part of the A20 had to be re-aligned to the north, to make room for the M20 extension to Folkestone.

Part of a full wall mural that could once be found inside the Star Inn. Stories vary about how it came into being. One story suggests that the mural was painted by a guest at The Star, in settlement of his account. Another, that it was created over time by an Irish artist who desired only food and drink in payment for his work. When demolition was threatened, there was much debate as to how this striking mural, thought to be the artist's only surviving work, could be saved.

The grill room of the Star Inn, in the mid 1970s with last orders about to be called in the pub. After the pub was pulled down, only the wall containing the mural remained standing in the hope that it might be reconstructed elsewhere. Sadly, it never was and only photographs survive today. However, a memory of the inn remains in the name Star Lane, close to junction twelve on the M20 at Cheriton.

Star Bridge, during demolition in March 1966 looking east towards Cheriton with the rooves of Cottage Homes just visible. To enable the superstructure to be removed, the A20 had to be diverted to the north of the bridge, on a route that took it down onto the old trackbed. This temporary route is seen under construction in the foreground. The bridge was finally despatched, albeit with great difficulty, using dynamite despite the close proximity of the Cottage Homes.

Sue Grundy holding her son Mark in front of an empty cottage, once known as School House, on 23 September 1978. School House stood at the rear of a large corner plot situated between Danton Lane and the A20. On the opposite side of the main road are Cottage Homes, the former orphanage and care home, and it is likely that School House was originally built as part of that complex. It was shortly demolished to make way for the M20 extension, which had begun two years previously.

Facing north along Danton Lane, in the mid 1980s, from the re-routed A20, as it approaches the Cheriton roundabout interchange with the M20. The A20's re-alignment north had halved the distance between its junction with Danton Lane and Danton Lane Cottages, nearest the camera. Also visible further to the north is the former Danton Farm complex, now The Dog Hotel. The oil seed rape crop, now going to seed, was one of the last to be grown in these fields.

A northwesterly view from the Cheriton Roundabout in late 1987. It shows the relationship between Peene (far left), Danton Pinch (right), the Dog Hotel in the foreground and the Cheriton Downs soaring up behind. By this time, much of the archaeological work was done, the old Danton Farm barn was mostly dismantled and all but one of the Danton Pinch residents had moved out. Within a year, only the downs and houses in Peene remained unchanged.

A panoramic view across the Seabrook Valley and westwards towards Beachborough, in the summer of 1988. All that remains of the Mill House are the excavated foundations, where archaeologists recently searched in vain for evidence of an earlier mill. Two little bridges survive over the Seabrook Stream, which would soon be covered over. The valley was then filled in with sand at this location. Visible to the right is the Beachborough to Frogholt stretch of the A20. The M20 is just off picture to the left.

Stone Farm post demolition, on 2 April 1988 looking west towards an, as yet, still intact Forge Cottage. The only traceable upstanding fragment of the house, was the lower part of the brick built lean-to coal and wood store, visible immediately in front of the tree. Remnants of Stone Farm's sixteenth century stone rubble ground floor walls are strewn about, although the majority of it had already been recovered. Soon, not even fragments or rubble would remain once construction of the access bridges had begun.

Facing west along what was once the Glebe Field, in mid to late 1988. Grubbed up trees, that once lined The Grove, are being gathered up for burning. Further back, grey piles of rubble are all that remains of Newington Grange and The Coach House. Surviving Newington properties, *Lone Pine* (centre) and *Skarthi*, recently re-named *Gore House* (right), are beyond the occupied territory. Forge Cottage is just visible at the far side of the A20 and would soon be a memory.

September 1988, another west facing view from a similar location as the one above. On the right, almost the entire area of the former Glebe Field is now occupied by a temporary re-alignment of the A20. This was done to allow construction of the three access bridges over the A20, without interrupting the traffic flow. The old route is still visible (left) with the area marked out ready for building work. The bungalow *Lone Pine* is now partially hidden behind a new fence line.

Burlington Field in September 1988, following demolition of the former rugby clubhouse. A breakdown in communications during the summer of 1986, led to both rugby club and Eurotunnel identifying different sites for the new grounds. However, it was quickly realized that Eurotunnel's chosen site, sandwiched between the M20 and existing railway line, could not even accommodate one rugby pitch, let alone two! Happily, by October 1986, both parties had agreed on a seven-acre site at Bargrove Farm, just south of Dollands Moor. Construction began in September 1987.

Longport from the southwest in May 1992, prior to a detailed architectural survey by Canterbury Archaeological Trust. In 1989, Eurotunnel finally bought the house and its one and a quarter-acre plot, because a site was needed for a police station. Once purchased, the house was boarded up, but nothing more done until the survey began. Until then, no decision had been reached about *Longport's* future and demolition was a considered option. Fortunately, the structural survey revealed a building of sufficient historical interest to justify preservation.

The front part of *Longport*, that is, the south facing cross wing, in May 1992. The survey found this to be the earliest phase, dating from the mid-sixteenth century. Originally, it followed the typical local pattern of stone rubble ground floor walls, with a jettied timber framed upper storey, topped by a hipped roof. As new, the building once extended further westwards (left), possibly into an open hall. This would explain the presence of the tiled gable end, rather than a hip, as at the east end (right).

The east elevation of *Longport* in spring 1992, with construction of the terminal all around it well advanced. The east end of the earlier building is to the left. The main range (right) was added to the back, or north elevation, of the original structure in the seventeenth century. The Canterbury Archaeological Trust's survey discovered that this later addition was, in fact, a late fourteenth century hall type house re-erected from elsewhere. The whole house was re-clad in red brick, probably in the eighteenth century, a fact that long hid *Longport's* true historical credentials.

Then: The approach to Newington from Frogholt in 1929, by which time work to create the A20 had just begun. The Old Forge is to the right, with the single storey smithy portion in the foreground. The notice on the steeply pitched roof reveals the blacksmith firm to be Kemsley & Son. To the left is Home Farm's malt house, with the junction for The Street, Newington in the middle distance. The west elevation of The Vicarage, later Newington Grange, can be glimpsed beyond a gap in the Scots Pines.

Now: The approach to Newington nearly seventy years later, with few comparable points of reference left. Both The Old Forge and malt house fell victim to road widening for the A20, completed here in 1932. Newington Grange ceded to the terminals road and rail access routes, which are carried over the A20 by three bridges. However, the junction for The Street is still in the same position, as is the bus stop (right), where passengers for Hythe wait, just as they did in the days of The Old Forge.

Then: A farm labourer with his two horse ploughing team, in the early years of the twentieth century. Behind, an impressive group of Cedar of Lebanon trees, does not quite obscure Stone Farm, the east end of which is just visible. To the right, the Ashford Road descends between high-sided banks, to a tight double bend around The Old Forge. The 'bottleneck' was eased by minor road improvements in about 1907, the same year that saw Frogholt by-passed by a new road.

Now: A Eurostar, recently arrived in England, slides across the nearest of three bridges over the A20 and towards Dollands Moor. Although the topography has changed completely, it would not be impossible to see horses at this location today. A bridle way emerges just in front of the bridge to the left and is picked up again on the other side, just before *Lone Pine* in The Street, Newington.

Then: An almost clandestine glance through the hedge at the east side of *Longport* in the mid 1980s. The house had long since ceased to be associated with a working farm. In the 1920s, Longport Farm was part of the Brockman Estate and the house occupied by a Major Salt. Then in the 1930s, the Vincents bought the farm and moved its milking duties to Home Farm at Newington.

Now: The new police station for the terminal, also called Longport, erected on the site of its predecessor. Construction work took just over a year to complete and it was officially opened by Countess Mountbatten on 3 March 1994. Some of the trees from the old farmhouse garden were preserved *in-situ* and now complement the new building. The old *Longport* was carefully dismantled and has found a new home at the Weald and Downland Museum at Singleton, Sussex.

Eight
Danton Lane and Farm

A poor quality, but unique view of the Cheriton Downs, by Robert Kennelly. The tall house nestling in the hillside was originally called *Northcliffe*, but later became better known as 'The Dolls House'. In the foreground is Hill Lane which then becomes the west to east section of Danton Lane. However, it is the north to south part of the lane, distinguished here by the hedgerow running from centre view to the right, that is the subject of this chapter.

Cadets from both the 12th Civil Service Volunteer Reserve and Bank of England Corps, march south along Danton Lane in 1906. They are passing an old barn and outbuildings belonging to Danton Farm. Northcliffe can just be made out, at the foot of the hills, in the distance. By this time, Danton Farm had ceased to be an independent working farm and was an out-station of the Brockman Estate, who then owned all the surrounding land.

The cadets continue past Danton Farm on their way back to Shorncliffe Camp in 1906. Behind, a woman stands outside the former farmhouse to Danton Farm. By now, it was the residence of the farm manager for the Brockman Estate, a job currently held by William Marchant. In about 1910, the Brockmans sold Danton Farm and all the surrounding land to Egerton Quested, after which, William Marchant lived briefly at Peene Bridge Farm, before buying The Old Vicarage at Newington in 1916.

The former Danton Farmhouse and surrounding buildings, in about 1927. The picture is by Paul Marchant, the youngest child of William Marchant's first marriage. He was born here in the 1890s, by which time the Marchants had four sons and two daughters, crammed into the limited space offered by the farmhouse. If that wasn't enough, the estate waggoner also lived at Danton Farm, in the upper room of the single-storey building, in the foreground of this photograph. He would join the family in the main house to take his meals.

Another view of Danton Farm by Paul Marchant, during the nostalgic visit to his birthplace, in the 1920s. The whole family had emigrated to Canada at the end of the 1890s, but returned after less than three years, because his mother Isabel was seriously ill and his father thought she would receive better care in England. Sadly, she died shortly after their return. Widower William Marchant, returned to his old job as Brockman's farm manager, and to Danton farmhouse, which had stood empty whilst they were abroad.

Eastgate, looking west across Danton Lane, on 27 February 1988, by which time it was empty and partly boarded up. As its name would imply, it is the easternmost property in Danton Pinch and the only one seen clearly from Danton Lane. The junction for Danton Pinch can just be seen far left, after which, Danton Lane passed through two tight ninety degree bends before resuming its course southwards.

The Danes in February 1988, looking south across Danton Lane, between the two aforementioned ninety degree bends. It was originally built as a flat roofed bungalow by Bert Mardle, to replace a derelict ragstone cottage. The pitched roof and extensions were added later. The property was named after the Mardle's two Great Danes, Paula and Freda, who were occasionally known to chase local children as they cycled past. There was a large plot associated with *The Danes*, part of which stretched along the south side of Danton Pinch.

Further south along the lane is *Broadlands*, built by Bert Mardle in about 1950, on the southernmost part of his large plot. He lived there himself after his first marriage broke up, but later sold it and returned to *The Danes*. The last residents, the Roberts family, experienced a disaster here early in their tenure. Mr Roberts was seriously injured in a boiler explosion, that was said to have blown him through the wall. When photographed in February 1988, *Broadlands* had become a squat for TML workers.

Looking back along Danton Lane in the bright sunshine of February 1988. The gable end of *Broadlands*'can be seen centre view and the roof of *Eastgate* far left. *The Danes* is obscured from view by the roof of *Broadlands*. The narrow twisting Danton Lane was used by the army, even in the later years. Sally Ivory remembers coming off her bike when suddenly encountering a fleet of army trucks coming round the tight bends by *The Danes*.

The east end of an early eighteenth century barn, at the former Danton Farm, in the mid 1980s. It was the oldest structure on the complex, but had seen changes over the years, most notably the provision of asbestos roofing to replace the Kent-Peg tiles. The history of Danton Farm during the years it was owned by Egerton Quested are unclear, but by 1940, it was derelict. However, it is known that an ancient threshing machine was stored in the barn for many years.

The former farmhouse seen from Danton Lane and across some outbuildings, in the mid 1980s. This view would not have been possible earlier in the century, as a tall pitched roof farm building once stood here. However, this had collapsed during the years of abandonment. Other damage incurred at this time included a fire that had destroyed part of the old barn, featured above. However, the old farmhouse was used briefly as headquarters for the 1st Cheriton Scouts in the late 1940s.

Another mid 1980s view, showing how Danton Lane passed through two more ninety degree bends to avoid the old farm complex. In recent years, articulated lorries had great problems negotiating these bends and would often hit the surrounding walls. The years of dereliction ended in about 1960, when the land was sold to Paul Tory and the former farm complex purchased by Mrs Joan Wright. After much repair and conversion work, she opened it as boarding kennels, called The Dog Hotel.

The Dog Hotel looking north from the lane in the mid 1980s. Comparison with early pictures shows that the south wall of the former farmhouse has lost its decorative scallop hung tiles in the intervening years. Dog Hotel owner Mrs Wright, sold the property to the Department of the Environment in 1974, when the government backed tunnel scheme was being mooted. However, when this fell through, the Dog Hotel was rented to Miss Betty Brown and Miss Joan Oakley for continued use as a boarding kennel.

Nos 1 and 2 Danton Lane Cottages, facing northeast in about 1986. The residents of No. 1, in the foreground, were June and Wilf Philpott, who had lived there since marrying in 1948. Before then, June Mayott as she was, lived with her family for a few years at No. 2. They had moved there from *Cliff End* in Danton Pinch. Danton Lane Cottages had been built in the 1900s, to prevent an extension to Folkestone Cemetery from being sited at Danton Lane.

School House, at the junction of Danton Lane and Cheriton High Street, in September 1978. Despite its official name, people usually referred to it by the name of the current occupant. To the rear was a low wall made of stone and brick. Wartime resident of No. 1 Danton Lane Cottages, Ian Warne, remembers lying on this wall as a child, to watch the aerial dog fights. In later years, it was occupied by the Foads, who had moved from No. 3a Danton Pinch.

An archaeology trench being examined in a field east of Danton Lane Cottages, during the summer of 1987. Such trenches were cut all over the designated terminal area. Those that yielded finds or evidence of occupation, would then be expanded and a more comprehensive dig begun. With regards to the cottages, mains services were late in coming. An electricity supply was connected in February 1964 and there was no indoor toilet or bathroom until 1966.

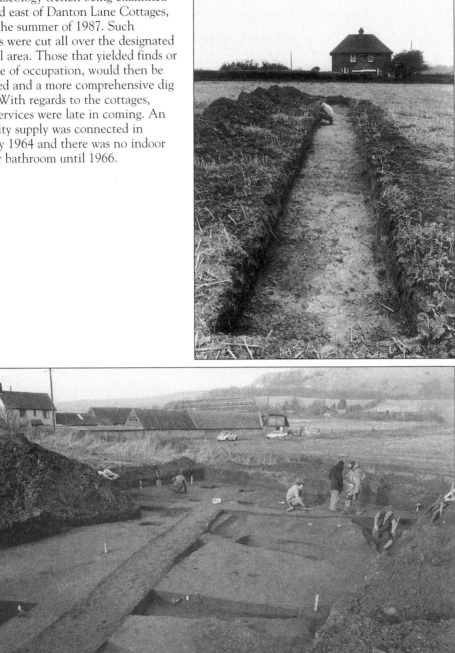

A major archaeological investigation in progress, east of the former Dog Hotel, in late 1987. Documentary research showed that Danton Farm had been built on the site of Dalmington, an ancient hamlet, so expectations were high that confirming evidence would be discovered. In the event, traces of human habitation from the late Anglo-Saxon period were discovered, in particular, a large wooden building thought to pre-date the hamlet of Dalmington.

The 250 year-old barn, once associated with Danton Farm, being dismantled by volunteers in late 1987. In June of that year, Eurotunnel offered to give the structure to the newly formed Elham Valley Line Trust, who sought local sponsors to pay for the cost of dismantling and moving it, estimated at approximately £6,000. A survey of the English oak timbers found them to be in reasonable condition, although some were rotten and others fire damaged. Dismantling of the barn would take six weeks, its re-erection at least that many years.

The closed Dog Hotel, stripped of its roof tiles, in late December 1987. Former occupants, Miss Brown and Miss Oakley, stood to lose both their home and business, if they could not find alternative premises. Eurotunnel had offered them land at both Newington and Peene, but in both cases, they were thwarted by Shepway District Council, who refused planning permission for kennels there, on the grounds of noise. They eventually found Eurotunnel owned accommodation at Sevington, Ashford, moving there on 17 December 1987. They were followed two days later by their canine guests.

Nos 2 and 1 Danton Lane Cottages on 27 February 1988, only days away from demolition. Already, all traces of the once well-kept gardens had been removed. No. 1 was boarded up, the Philpotts had long gone. Norman and Christine Hall had purchased No. 2 in 1970, then sold to the Department of the Environment in 1974, when the earlier 'Chunnel' scheme was proposed. Since then, they had rented the house and raised a family there.

A sad sight for the families who had spent many happy years at Danton Lane Cottages. It was March 1988 and the work of the demolition gang was well advanced. The same month saw the clearance of the former Dog Hotel buildings and the bungalow *Broadlands*, although *The Danes* was probably pulled down with the Danton Pinch properties a few months later.

Naturalist Leigh Gillett looks along the truncated remains of the top end of Danton Lane, in September 1988. Wires hang aimlessly from the electricity pole, the houses it served now part of history. The stump end of the lane soon became a well known spot for dumping rubbish, to such an extent that people started visiting there to see what they could find!

Danton Lane, curving around the empty and stripped buildings of the Dog Hotel, at the end of December 1987. Once the old barn had gone into store, the only other thing considered worth saving were the roof tiles. By this time, archaeological work on the main terminal area was winding down, although a watching presence was maintained during the initial stripping and levelling of the landscape.

Danton Farm April 1988 from the same location and the old complex is no more. Although the landscape was changing rapidly, lorries continued to follow the course of Danton Lane, with its telegraph poles still in place. In May, Eurotunnel applied for planning permission to install a temporary caravan park on the former farm and Dog Hotel site. The TML workers who lived there would be the last inhabitants of Danton Lane.

The bottom end of Danton Lane, at its junction with the A20, in September 1988. Now it was merely one of a number of access points onto a vast construction site. Security here was very tight, as is evident from the road barrier and warning signs. This was in marked contrast to the situation at the top end of the lane, where nothing prevented anyone from wandering onto the site!

Then: Three Austin Seven Ruby Saloons and an unknown chassis, in the grounds of *The Danes*, looking south on Saturday 9 December 1967. Collecting these vehicles was one of Bert Mardle's many interests and the ones he acquired were not wrecks, nor were they runners either! Paul Grundy, who was restoring an Austin Seven himself at the time, called on Bert in a fruitless search for spares and took this photograph as a souvenir of his visit.

Now: The first of two overbridges, allowing vehicular access onto the shuttle platforms via ramps, which slope away from it to the left. The railway tracks that it spans have just emerged from the north portal of the loop tunnel (right), through which all arriving shuttle trains make a 180 degree turn before unloading and reloading. It is sad to reflect that unlike Bert Mardle's collection of old Austins once parked on this very spot, few British made cars will now pass this way.

Then: Mr C.P. Davis, of the Folkestone and District Local History Society, looks northwards along Danton Lane on a late spring day in the mid 1980s. The photographer is standing at the beginning of a footpath which leads across the fields in a southeasterly direction towards Cheriton. The amount of asbestos roof sheeting needed on the buildings of the Dog Hotel, is testament to the state of disrepair that Danton Farm had fallen into prior to 1960.

Now: The north side of the terminal's service and maintenance area, in April 1998. The pre-fabricated structure is called Danton House, to acknowledge the fact that it occupies the site of the old Danton Farm. Behind it, an embankment carries the continental main line, on which Eurostars and freight trains pass through the terminal area. Since this picture was taken, Danton House has been dismantled and the last link with the past, albeit only in name, has now gone.

Then: The grounds of No. 2, Danton Lane Cottages, in the mid 1980s, facing south towards Cheriton. Curly the donkey, seen to the left of the caravan, is the twenty year-old pet of the Hall family. When eviction was looming in the latter half of 1987, a major concern for the family was that they be re-housed in a place with suitable grazing for Curly. Finally, just two weeks before Christmas, Eurotunnel offered the Halls a four bedroomed house at Peene, with grounds that could accommodate Curly.

Now: The south side of the terminal's service area, adjacent to the maintenance shed. It is sad to reflect that the graves of Wilfred and June Philpott's pets are now beneath this concrete surface. Just beyond the parking area is the approach to the south portal of the loop tunnel (right), used by all shuttle trains. In the distance can be seen the Eurotunnel Administration Building and to the left of it, the roof of the Cottage Homes, the only common factor in both 'then' and 'now' views.

Nine
En Route to
Caesar's Camp

Trenches being cut by Canterbury Archaeological Trust, east of Danton Lane, in September 1987. Such trenches appeared all over the 500-acre terminal site. The vast majority yielded nothing except undisturbed natural deposits, usually an indication of an uninhabited area. However much later, it was realized that soil deposits, washing down from the Cheriton Hills over the centuries, would have covered some early settlement sites. Therefore, had the trenches been cut deeper, then more information may have been discovered.

A panoramic view of the heart of the designated terminal area, from the Cheriton Downs, in late 1987. Biggins Wood can be seen centre left and to its right, a continuous line of downhill trenches are arranged to facilitate drainage. Many such panoramic views were documented by local walkers. Peter Hooper documented such panoramic views, over the next few years, as the terminal construction progressed. Archaeologists found the remains of an Anglo-Saxon structure north-west of Biggins Wood, from which a Roman brooch was recovered.

A southeast facing view of Biggins Wood in the mid 1980s; which consisted of many oak trees. TML refrained from clearing the woodland until September 1988, to avoid the bird nesting season. After the trees had been felled the top soil, rich in seeds and insect life, was deposited on a site at the foot of Cheriton Hill, now known as New Biggins Wood.

Caesar's Camp from a site just south of the Biggins Wood area, in April 1988. The A20 diversion, opened in 1981, is immediately to the right. In the foreground is a concrete culvert that takes one of the areas many small streams beneath the new road. The deep track marks leading across the crop-less fields, were made by excavators carrying out trenching, a task completed by this time.

The road leading to the Folkestone Waterworks and Reservoirs, northwest of Castle Hill and Caesar's Camp in April 1988. The area immediately in the foreground, is where the Channel Tunnel portal would be situated. However, to allow continued access to the waterworks, its approach road would first need to be taken underground in a long thin concrete tunnel, before the trackbed could be prepared and the portal constructed.

A northwesterly view of the eastern extremity for the planned terminal area in 1986 from the small roundabout, where the 1981 A20 diversion meets Cherry Garden Avenue coming up from Folkestone and Castle Hill and down from Crete Road West. In a few years to come, the M20 motorway was extended to terminate at this point. The small roundabout gave way to a double roundabout junction complex, designated Junction 13 of the M20.

An interesting scene facing west from halfway up Caesar's Camp, in April 1988. Below, two vehicles are parked in Castle Hill and beyond them, the portal area where test boring is taking place. At the top of the picture is the waterworks approach road, featured earlier. Many trees in this area had been cleared in 1987, to allow for the preparatory work.

Then: An easterly study of wheat ripening in the vast acreage west of Caesar's Camp and south of Cherry Garden Hill, in the mid 1980s. The last crops of oil seed rape and wheat were harvested in the summer of 1987, with the archaeologists virtually following the combine harvesters. As is the case all over Kent, these 'prairies' once existed as a series of smaller fields, enclosed by Hawthorn hedges. The loss of these hedgerows, together with the reduction of Biggins Wood, is systematic of modern farming methods.

Now: The same scene today, from the terminal's south service road. The view of Caesar's Camp is interrupted by the easternmost of two bridges, that carry the exit roads up from the shuttle platforms and over the tracks (and the service road), to the main customer exit route. In the distance, a freight shuttle train is departing the terminal and heading for the English portal of the Channel Tunnel.

Then: Cherry Garden Hill, in April 1988, facing northeast from a field on the eastern side of Biggins Wood. The edge of Caesar's Camp is just visible to the right. In the foreground, abandoned linear trenches are now full of water. Archaeological investigations closer to Cherry Garden Hill turned up some rubbish pits dating back to approximately AD 725, indicating the existence of a nearby Anglo-Saxon settlement.

Now: Exactly ten years later and a departing freight shuttle crosses the foot of Cherry Garden Hill. It can be identified as a freight shuttle by the presence of a passenger coach behind the leading locomotive. This is provided for lorry drivers who, unlike car and coach travellers, cannot remain with their vehicles. Just out of shot (left) is the Main Intake Sub Station, or 'Miss UK' for short. The counterpart at the French terminal is known, of course, as 'Miss France'.

Ten

Construction Begins

Clearance for the terminal approaches, immediately south east of Newington in spring 1988. The churned up area in the foreground was Glebe Field and the trees that once lined The Grove, have now been grubbed up. Beyond The Grove (right) and yet untouched, is Vicarage Meadow, with its railway wagon animal shelter. Further back and beyond the trees, is one of the pitches for Folkestone Rugby Club, its goal posts still in place.

September 1988 and a shattered railway wagon, once used as a stable for ponies, is the only trace left of Vicarage Meadow. Behind the wagon, the rugby pitches have gone, to be replaced by deep excavations for what will become the shuttle train loop tunnel.

The massive semi-circular excavation for the loop tunnel, immediately east of Newington in October 1988. Left is a recently erected garden fence for the Newington property *Shelton* and it becomes clear just how close the loop tunnel is to some village homes! The tunnel will be used by all incoming shuttle trains to make a 180 degree turn before entering the platform area.

The village of Newington, facing north across the A20, in October 1988. Left is the Police House, on a site once occupied by the old malt house. The church is also visible beyond. At the junction with The Street, a notice warns : 'No TML works traffic beyond this point'. The site in the foreground, once occupied by Forge Cottage and Stone Farm's outbuildings, is being prepared for temporary pumping operations.

Facing west at the void between the M20 (right) and the A20, part of which is just visible to the left. Cylindrical bridge piers are already in place either side of the motorway. Those in the foreground will carry the exit road from the terminal, whereas the quartet beyond them will support the bridge for the 'Continental Main Line'.

Cranes pile-driving for the bridge supports, to carry road and rail access over the A20, viewed from the calm of Newington churchyard, in October 1988. What would the incumbents of this peaceful oasis, such as Jack Heyman and the Vincents, think of the changed landscape around them now?

A convoy of earth graders and bulldozers, about to plough through escapees from the last crop of oil seed rape, in summer 1988. Archaeologists continued to maintain a presence during this land levelling process, in case something significant was unearthed. Behind the machines is the Elham Valley Railway embankment, its slopes already stripped to reveal the chalk core, mined from Eachendhill just over a hundred years before.

A section of the thirty-inch diameter, three-mile long pipeline, being carried over the A20, during construction in September 1988. This was laid from Seabrook to the terminal site, and was soon ready to pump an estimated 500 million cubic metres of sand and water onto it. The sand was used to complete the levelling process and provide a stable foundation for construction work. The old house *Longport* is just visible through the hedge.

Eurotunnel's £2 million Exhibition Centre under construction in early September 1988. Later that month it was officially opened by Trade and Industry Secretary, Lord Young. Eurotunnel were obliged to provide a visitor and information centre as a condition of the Channel Tunnel Act. It was expected to attract up to 300,000 visitors per year, for the duration of the terminal construction. Amongst the displays was a massive working model of the completed terminal complex.

A panoramic view across the terminal area, from the site offices east of Danton Lane, in about August 1988. In the middle distance a heavy plant digger is engaged in the process of site levelling. Beyond and to the right, caravans for TML workers occupy the sites of the demolished Danton Lane properties *Broadlands* and *The Danes*. To their left, all of the Danton Pinch properties have gone, but remains of some of the outbuildings to *Its-It*, can just be made out.

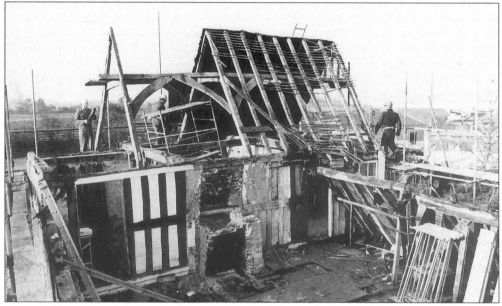

Longport being dismantled in November 1992, prior to its move to the Weald and Downland Museum at Singleton. Here, staff from the museum, with Canterbury Archaeological Trust, dismantle the sixteenth century roof timbers of the cross wing, the oldest part of the house. During this process, every timber member had to be numbered prior to removal. The same applied to nearly 9,000 bricks! This meticulous work required much concentration, but could also be quite physically demanding.

Then: The south portal of the loop tunnel, facing northwest from the security fence along the A20, in December 1990. The cutting is wide here, in order to accommodate both tunnel approaches and stabling lines for out of service shuttle trains. The loop tunnel had to be finished early, so that work on the terminal could commence above it. Far left, is the east elevation of *Longport*, its lower windows already boarded up, denoting its empty state.

Now: A shuttle train enters the loop tunnel, its rear locomotive partially obscured by the screen of tree saplings planted along the site perimeter. Within a few minutes, it will emerge on the north side of the terminal, facing in the right direction to enter the platform area and then return to Calais. *Longport* has been replaced by the police station complex, but the pylon remains unmoved. Far right, the gantry across the toll area can just be seen.

Then: Facing west from Caesar's Camp, across the lush broad leafed trees and ripening crops of the 500-acre area, soon to become the Channel Tunnel Terminal. It is the calm before the storm in the summer of 1986, although to the bottom of the photograph, just off Castle Hill, test boring near the designated portal area has already begun. The waterworks approach road is hidden by trees, as are the slopes to Cherry Garden Hill beyond. Further still, is the oak dominated Biggins Wood, which may be described as the lungs of Cheriton.

Now: The terminal, all but completed, in December 1992. The service road snakes its way over the portal and down to the terminal's fire station (left). Beyond, the tracks are laid and platforms ready to receive the first shuttle train. However, the Eurostar service that rushed through unconcerned was the first train to use the tunnel. Today, tree saplings planted around the terminal perimeter, help to soothe the wounds of the construction work, but cannot compensate for the way it was before the Channel Tunnel.